YOUR KNOWLEDGE HAS VALUE

- We will publish your bachelor's and master's thesis, essays and papers

- Your own eBook and book - sold worldwide in all relevant shops

- Earn money with each sale

Upload your text at www.GRIN.com
and publish for free

Bibliographic information published by the German National Library:

The German National Library lists this publication in the National Bibliography; detailed bibliographic data are available on the Internet at http://dnb.dnb.de .

This book is copyright material and must not be copied, reproduced, transferred, distributed, leased, licensed or publicly performed or used in any way except as specifically permitted in writing by the publishers, as allowed under the terms and conditions under which it was purchased or as strictly permitted by applicable copyright law. Any unauthorized distribution or use of this text may be a direct infringement of the author s and publisher s rights and those responsible may be liable in law accordingly.

Imprint:

Copyright © 2016 GRIN Verlag, Open Publishing GmbH
Print and binding: Books on Demand GmbH, Norderstedt Germany
ISBN: 9783668333932

This book at GRIN:

http://www.grin.com/en/e-book/343570/the-national-style-of-japanese-films-by-the-1930s

Ian Akbar

The 'National Style' of Japanese films by the 1930s

GRIN Publishing

GRIN - Your knowledge has value

Since its foundation in 1998, GRIN has specialized in publishing academic texts by students, college teachers and other academics as e-book and printed book. The website www.grin.com is an ideal platform for presenting term papers, final papers, scientific essays, dissertations and specialist books.

Visit us on the internet:

http://www.grin.com/

http://www.facebook.com/grincom

http://www.twitter.com/grin_com

The 'National Style' of Japanese Films by the 1930s

An examination of Japanese film history up until the 1930s reveals striking differences to that of the West. Silent films were the first variety of films to be shown in the 1890s, as they were in many countries. These films were largely influenced by the traditional Japanese performing art known as *kabuki*, which had a huge influence on films of this period, as did other forms of art. Intrinsic to these early silent films was the presence of a physical narrator, the *benshi*. The *benshi* both resisted and had a lasting influence on sound films which began to be produced in the 1930s. In addition to the above, this paper will endeavour to demonstrate how Japanese cultural perceptions influenced the use of cinematic techniques largely derived from the West and produced a "national style" of film by the 1930s. In order to facilitate this discussion, Japanese film styles, the influence of reform and culture and exactly how cinematic techniques were put to different uses, as compared to the West, will be examined.

The first type of motion picture in Japan was the silent film of the 1890s. Burch (1979, 490) mentions that "the Japanese silent film was the most silent of all", due to the absence of speech (i.e., no one was actually "speaking" in the film). Speech was explicitly absent, since it was put aside. A voice was present outside the film, detached from the images themselves, images in which the actors were confined to static visual representations of the scenes unfolding through the voice, like the dolls or the *kabuki* actors of the Edo stage. The silent era came to an end in the late 1930s. Sadao Yamanaka is citied as having been the leading figure in this type of filmmaking in the 1930s when "talkies" or sound films slowly replaced silent films (Kung Fu Cinema, 2004).

In relation to the influence of traditional Japanese performing arts, according to Burch (1979, 495), the vast majority of films in Japan up until the 1930s, were inspired by *kabuki*, or from its' derivatives, *shimpa* and *shin-kabuki* (modernized kabuki). Burch (1979, 495) states that the "*visual* traits of kabuki appeared constantly on the screen". Burch points out that the visual traits of *kabuki* helped to preserve the Japanese cinema against Western 'realism'. "The stylized fighting sequences in which no actual blows were exchanged, the use of the backward somersault signifying the death of a fighter, the translation into Melies-like 'special effects' of the transformational machinery of *kabuki* and, above all, the action-stopping *mie*, or *tableau vivant* (which terminates most of the scenes of Makino's early *Chushingura*), were clear 'distancing devices' which needed no special elucidation" (Burch 1979, 495) for the Japanese audience due to their familiarity with *kabuki*.

Film was also perceived differently in Japan. Richie (1990, 409/409) notes that due to the influence of the *kabuki* theatre, early film performances were thought of as a new kind of drama and thus were expected to be theatrical since the cinema was considered an extension of the stage. Cinema was not thought of as a new kind of photography as it was in the West. Therefore, all drama had to be 'presented'. While dramatic situations were represented on the stage, they were also to be presented simultaneously by an authoritative voice. Riche (1990, 409) states that in a Japanese film the authoritative voice was the *benshi*, "a person who, in addition to satisfying theatrical expectations, explained, commented upon, and made the parts of the film into a coherent whole. This authoritative voice was necessary because imported films were composed of foreign scenes, and these new sights had to be interpreted, commented upon and translated into terms comprehensible to the audience." Burch (1979, 517) adds that the *benshi* spelled out the diegesis (i.e., narration) of films throughout the 1920s and well into the 1930s.

Accordingly Richie (1990, 411) states that Japan was criticised that its' early films were nothing but vehicles for the *benshi*. It was true that the *benshi* worked best with a cinema which was stage-like, where actors were distant from the camera, long takes were made, and editing was done in a simple connective sense. Anderson (1982, 466) notes, however, that before 1920, "many movies made directly from *Shimpa* or Kabuki plays did not use solo *benshi*". Many movies utilized a type of live dubbing performed by a group of actors or *benshi*, hidden behind the screen or beside it in plain view. This voicing technique was called moving-picture *kowairo* and was directly adopted from traditional *kowairo*. Anderson (1982, 467) goes on to state that since the new 1920s style Japanese films drove out the *kowairo* and chain drama forms, which were easily the dominant forms of narrative in the Japanese theater during the 1910s, the position of the solo *benshi* was strengthened.

Further change, however, produced a threat to the institution of the *benshi*. Due to the threat to his livelihood, the *benshi* naturally resisted modernization in the cinema. Burch (1979, 489) points out that the *benshi* "fought bitterly against the introduction of new narrative structures such as the flashback". Burch (1979, 517) also mentions that since new-style directors universally disliked the *benshi* as representative of the old style, it is assumed that the abundance of inter-titles within early films, both descriptive and "spoken", represented attempts to set limits on the *benshi* and "to channel his reading in accordance with the notions of unity and linearity [i.e., the ordered sequence of events in time] which were inevitably a part of the process of Westernization." It appears, however, that the *benshi* rebelled by digressing as far as possible from the screen text (i.e., by adding additional or extra information) even while it was being projected on the screen.

However, from the Japanese perspective, the *benshi* played a major role in ensuring linearity in films up until the 1930s. Richie (1990, 414) and Burch (1979, 508) both note that "since neither physical or psychological depth was sought [in Japanese films], the kind of narrative tightness so prized in the West is not found in the Japanese films." The idea that each scene should propel the story through to its conclusion was not one to which Japanese literature, drama or film subscribed. Rather, separate scenes were devoted to separate events (e.g., the flights of lovers, the soliloquy, the recognition scene, etc.). These scenes might halt the narrative but they also contained, for the Japanese audience moments of beauty, contemplation, and familiarity, which they found appropriate and satisfying. Stories could be fragmented due to the unifying voice of the *benshi*.

Richie (1990, 410/411) notes that the *benshi* flourished for nearly thirty years, until the advent of the sound film. To this day the *benshi*'s influence "is still manifest in the superfluous explanation often encountered in Japanese films, the presentation rather than the representation of an emotion, and the sudden, direct commentary – for example, that disembodied voice in the middle of Kurosawa's *Ikiru*. In addition, the common voice-over which detaches audiences from emotion, the spoken meditation which creates the elegiac mood, the pronouncement which lends a feeling of inevitability – all these are also part of the legacy of the *benshi*."

In terms of film style, as the reader will see below, Richie (2001, 435) iterates that David Bordwell identified three examples of Japanese-style cinema narrative. The 'calligraphic' style, was associated with *chambara* (Japanese sword-fighting), and was flamboyant, full of fast action, rapid editing, and bravura camera. Second was the 'pictorialist' style, derived from *shimpa* and influenced by Hollywood's Josef von Sternberg, in which each shot was a complex composition with long shots predominating. Third, was the 'piecemeal' style (one bit of information per shot), where the average shot length ranged from three to five seconds, and the narrative was associated with *gendaigeki* (i.e., a genre of television, theatre and films focusing on the Edo Period, 1600 – 1870) and influenced by Lubitsch.

In relation to *shimpa*, Burch (1979, 481) states that *shimpa* "catered to the newly urbanized peasants of the Meiji period (1868-1912), and *shin-geki* (modern theatre), which was a direct expression of the struggle of the liberal bourgeoisie and indirectly of the embryonic working-class movement was a further step." *Shimpa* (new school) largely featured tragic stories involving women. (Midnight Eye, 2001) Burch (1979, 487) also mentions that *chambara* (old school) or swordplay films, derived from *kabuki*, monopolized the screen during the latter part of the silent era (1920 to 1936). In addition, Burch (1979, 522) posits that *chambara* was the result of a meeting between Japanese presentationalism and Western modes of representation and realism. The main difference between the earliest *chambara* and *shimpa* plays was the greater realism of the sword-fights.

In addition, Richie (2001, 444) mentions that during the same period that the *gendaigeki* was being developed from the *shimpa*, "the new jidaigeki was being fashioned from the old kabuki-based kyuha (i.e., period dramas)". The driving force behind the new period-film was the *shinkokugeki*, or "new national drama". The *shinkokugeki* appeared in 1917 and featured more literal violence and realism in *jidaigeki* than did the kyuha. The term "*geki*" literally means theater and *jidaigeki* generally refers to all Japanese movies set before 1868, when Japan's modern era began with the Meiji Restoration. Within this broad title lies three sub-genres including the *sengoku jidai* that depicts Sengoku period films (1490 – 1600), the *ken geki* or sword fighting films that are also known as *chambara* films, and the *yakuza geki* or gangster films. Motion pictures were played in Japan as early as 1897, but it wasn't until 1923 that the term *jidaigeki* came into being. (Kung Fu Cinema, 2004) Anderson (1982, 472) states that *jidaigeki* was characterized by repetitious visual compositions which held the eye.

According to Burch (1979, 537/538), in the 1920s in Japan, a few film makers called for reform of the Japanese cinema. These filmmakers represented the needs of the middle class struggling to achieve dominant status and the return to the values of feudal Japan in the films of the 1930s. However, since this rising class required more realism in film than was previously evident and because the West had produced such a system, Japanese directors understandably adopted it. These directors were all the more drawn to this new system of cinematic representation because it was opposed to the traditional mode in every way. The reason these directors so strongly rejected the traditional mode was because it was so intimately bound up with the dominant class of "feudal capitalists" who still controlled Japan.

Reform produced a change which was contrary to established tradition of the time. Richie (2001, 458) states that "one of the results of *Seisaku's Wife* (1924) was more real females playing women on screen". The *oyama* or *onnagata* (i.e., female impersonator), who had played the role of women to this point, "had by now all but disappeared, and actresses were becoming popular. Among these were Uemura Yoko, Sawamura Haruko (who had appeared in *Souls on the Road*) and – most popular of all – Kurishima Sumiko, whose photographs were best-sellers." The result was that more women began to go to the movies, which meant a new audience to be satisfied. This occurrence produced a separate genre, which was referred to as the "women's picture" to differentiate it from men's pictures, the *jidageki*.

As has been demonstrated above, the Japanese film up until the 1930s was largely influenced by traditional Japanese culture and perspective. Richie (2001, 445/446) notes that director Masumura Yasuzo stated that, from the 1920s on, *kodan*, a storytelling format – with its abbreviated statements, curt dialogue, and swift shifts of scene – exerted a major influence on the structure of *jidaigeki*. The acting consisted of lots of facial expressions plus influences from William S. Hart, and Douglas Fairbanks. The new sword-fighting samurai was an individual, even a nonconformist, a kind of kimonoed cowboy. This type identified with the *tateyaku*, a term taken from *kabuki* to represent idealized samurai, warriors who were not only victorious in battle but also wise, determined men, with strong wills. Moreover, Richie (2001, 449) mentions that the *jidaigeki* were sometimes based on traditional prints (e.g., *ukiyoe*), which "dramatized scene and encapsulated story". One scene followed the other, its impetus not so much owed to storyline as to aesthetic spectacle.

However, unity in sound film plot and narrative was achieved through an accommodation between the traditions of the East and the West. According to Richie (2001, 434) "Japanese filmmakers borrowed extensively from native popular literature, from the theater's reworkings of Western narrative principles and from foreign (particularly American) films' conventions of style and structure." Richie (1990, 418) mentions that *Souls on the Road* (Rojo no reikon, 1921) was the picture which for many marks the true beginning of the Japanese cinema. Richie (1990, 420) goes on to state that it was "the first film to illustrate the hybrid nature of the Japanese cinematic style and to indicate how accommodation could be turned into strengths. *Souls on the Road* displayed Western style to an extreme. The film began and ended with a literary quotation (a short passage from *The Lower Depths*). "The young daughter of the house, hair in long ringlets was dressed to look like Mary Pickford and acted like her. The action took place on

Christmas Eve, an 'exotic' festival to the Japanese, at the time. There were all sorts of devices such as wipes, fades, dissolves and irises, noticeable intercutting among the stories (no matter that such *Intolerance*-like editing is, to the Western eye, in no way appropriate to the slightness of the domestic tragedies involved), as well as a number of close-ups (bust-shots)." However, Richie (1990, 421) also posits that despite its Western influences, *Souls on the Road* was very Japanese as it displayed the distinctive Japanese linear style, which was constantly disrupted.

Regarding presentation, Richie (2001, 433/434) also points out that particularly "Japanese" is an eleven-minute episode in *A Star Athlete (*Hanagata senshu, 1937), where thirty consecutive dolly movements were used: "forward or backward along a country road, with the camera always preceding or following the students." Of this sequence, Allen Stanbrook has also said that "by subtly varying the angles, now dollying forward, now dollying back, now marching at the double or letting the camera break free to follow, [Hiroshi] Shimizu created a sequence close to pure cinema in which the matter of the film is almost subservient to the form." This technique could be found in the usage of space exemplified in *e-maki*, a painted handscroll where space is unrolled (unreeled) before the viewer. It was also during that sequence that two marching students compared their situation with that of Gary Cooper in *Morocco* – an example of Shimizu's fusing of Eastern and Western concerns.

In addition, according to Burch (1979, 497), Japanese films up to the 1930s displayed a certain "flatness" which was derived from *kabuki* and the doll theatre. This "flatness" was apparently the general rule in the early films and was a trait which endured into the 1920s, "and left an indelible mark on the films of some of the masters of the 1930s". Burch (1979, 529) notes that this was caused by a "general lack of concern with visual depth in the arts of the East and particularly those of Japan (*e-makimono,* or picture scrolls, Muromachi screens, the prints of *ukiyo-e, no, kabuki,* doll theatre) were preserved in cinema long after the 'laws' of depth-representation by the camera were established in the West." Moreover, Richie (1990, 415) mentions that Japanese films of this period were also characterized by a "high regard for convention and a relatively low regard for originality". This meant that clichés were endlessly repeated and stereotypes welcomed (e.g., falling cherry blossoms for doomed lovers, dark glasses for bad foreigners, etc.).

It is apparent that cinematic techniques were used for different purposes from East to West, driven by cultural preference. Richie (1990, 417) iterates that foreign techniques such as close-ups, shorter takes and logical narrative began to be utilized for functions similar to those in Western films. At the same time these elements, of foreign style, were altered. Burch (1979, 494) also notes that Japanese cinema was not interested in Western styles as a system, merely as an occasional tool to produce special dramatic effects.

Richie (2001, 442) also notes that other lessons learned from American films were sound effects and background music, which were constantly used. Another American lesson, according to Richie, was a super-active camera which always sought ways to express itself. One of the best examples was in Mikio Naruse's, *Two Wives,* where there was a very high shot from over a wisteria trellis, by way of an aerial dolly, which showed the interiors of several rooms of Kimiko's (the heroine of the picture) house, but had no other justification.

Lastly, in relation to films displayed on television, (i.e., from the 1970s) Burch (1979, 533) states that in the sound film of the West, super-inscription was a common feature in credit titles and scroll prologues, and represented an intermediate stage between 'reality' and full absorption in the narrative. In the Japanese film, the narrative was not taboo since the *benshi* had already been "writing on it" (i.e., commenting on films). As Burch (1979, 533) notes, "even today, this relative indifference towards one of the vital premises of Western illusionism is instanced daily on commercial television channels, since at any moment, particularly during peak viewings, in the midst of the most thoroughly encoded gangster serial or samurai drama, large, often ingeniously animated characters may invade the lower portion of the screen to remind us of the merits of a deodorant or a Korean barbecues."

It is clear that the Japanese film up until the 1930s displayed a very characteristic "national style" which was very different from the West. Cinematic techniques were used in different ways and for different purposes. Such items as visual depth and linearity were also construed and presented differently as were the diegesis itself. Early reform of the Japanese film industry, in addition, to making film more realistic and accessible for the working classes also allowed women to participate in film and for an entirely new genre of film to be created focused on the fairer sex. The influence of Japanese traditional arts, in particular the performing art of *kabuki*, certainly cannot be under emphasized. *Kabuki* was the inspiration for the *chambara*, a very Japanese film style, as well as the presence of the authoritative voice of the *benshi* in the early silent films of this period. The influence of the dramatic and visual arts has had a lasting influence on Japanese films up until the 1930s and has played a large part in the characteristic "national style" of Japanese film.

Bibliography

Anderson, Joseph, 1982, "Second and third thoughts about the Japanese film" In: Richie, Donald and Anderson, Joseph *The Japanese Film* in CIJ 421: Cultural Contact and Hybridity in the Arts in Asia, Resource Book. University of New England, Armidale, NSW. Pp. 439 – 41.

Burch, Noel, 1979, *To the Distant Observer: Form and Meaning in the Japanese Cinema* in CIJ 421: Cultural Contact and Hybridity in the Arts in Asia, Resource Book. University of New England, Armidale, NSW. Pp. 67 – 139.

Gerow, Aaron, 2000, "Screening the Past: One print in the age of mechanical reproduction: film industry and culture in 1910s Japan". Retrieved on October 24, 2004 from http://www.latrobe.educ.au/screeningthepast/firstrelease/fr1100/agfr11e.htm

Kung Fu Cinema, 2004, "Jidai Geki – Introduction". Retrieved on Oct. 11, 2004 from http://www.kungfucinema.com/categories/jidaigeki.htm

Midnight Eye, 2001, "Forgotten Fragments: An Introduction to Japanese Silent Cinema". Retrieved on Oct. 24, 2004 from http://www.midnighteye.com/features/silentfilm_pt2.shtml

Richie, Donald, 2001, "Taisho democracy and Shochiku". *A Hundred Years of Japanese Film* in CIJ 421: Cultural Contact and Hybridity in the Arts in Asia, Resource Book. University of New England, Armidale, NSW. Pp. 43 – 84.

Richie, Donald, 1990, "From the beginnings to the early 1920s" *Japanese Cinema: An Introduction* in CIJ 421: Cultural Contact and Hybridity in the Arts in Asia, Resource Book. University of New England, Armidale, NSW. Pp.1 – 16.

YOUR KNOWLEDGE HAS VALUE

- We will publish your bachelor's and master's thesis, essays and papers

- Your own eBook and book - sold worldwide in all relevant shops

- Earn money with each sale

Upload your text at www.GRIN.com
and publish for free